Women
Must
Save the World!

A Call to Action

Published by Alouette Enterprises, Inc.

2020 Donna Fridrych
All rights reserved.

ISBN: 978-0-9797577-0-9

Printed in the USA

Dedication

To all the women in the world today

Introduction

This is a short book with an urgent message. It's a call for women to assume leadership at this time of global crisis. The book makes two main points:

The world must start operating like a global family

Women must lead the change to create this new world

My appeal in this book is for women to provide overall leadership for businesses and governments around the world. This may sound radical or extreme to some readers. But as a global society, we have reached a point where extreme measures are needed. It is time for a radical change from years of the patriarchal model of leadership that has brought us to the brink of societal, economic, and environmental collapse. The Covid-19 pandemic and the catastrophic effects of global warming are tipping points—final warning signs that we, as global citizens, should heed. To steer this planet onto a new and positive course, we need leadership that respects and promotes the best interests of everyone on this earth—women's leadership.

Women Must Save the World! is not a feminist pitch for equality. I will not argue that women deserve greater opportunities for leadership roles. That's old news. Despite making strides in recent decades to fill leadership positions in the developed nations of the world, women remain underrepresented at the top levels of business and government. As a former executive and consultant, I speak from experience. Patriarchy and male privilege still rule the day. Corporate interests and greed continue to influence decisions at the expense of people and the environment.

The purpose of this book is to show why women are better able than men to lead the planet to safety and prosperity. What we need today are leadership skills that most women inherently possess—relationship building, compassion, creativity, teamwork, and holistic thinking. While masculine bravado and brawn may have worked in centuries past, women today are uniquely positioned to lead because of their education and skills.

The shift to women's leadership proposed in this book does not aim to discredit men or eliminate their participation. Empowered, farsighted men are encouraged to join in and help create this new world. However, the key to its success will be to eliminate the patriarchal mindset that has led us down the path of continuous warfare, terrorism, environmental destruction, human rights violations, and every atrocity imaginable.

To put our current world situation into perspective, I first look at how we got to this point in history. I provide an overview of the scale of global warfare since World War I, and show how the warlike mentality of the ruling patriarchy has dominated government and corporate leadership. Today we see many threatening signs that demand new leadership: twenty wars around the globe; tensions mounting between the superpowers; an increase in white supremacist movements; riots and looting because of racial injustices … the list goes on.

I examine women's climb to leadership roles and explain why it is women who are best qualified to lead the transformation of our society into a global family. I also provide some guidelines and a framework for how a new global family could be realized. In this vision and model, businesses and governments not only would be responsible for providing basic necessities but would also serve to enhance the lives of everyone around the world. All of this is doable with new leadership, a change in mindset, and the reallocation of money currently invested in perpetuating warfare, protectionism, and domination.

At the end of the book, I explain how you, the reader, can participate in creating a global family by first examining your own biases and prejudices. We must look within and open our hearts and minds to help support the change we wish to see in our world. I also give you the opportunity to nominate women of your choice to serve in leadership roles as consultants and help us transition to a new world led by women.

Thank you in advance for your participation in helping women to stand up and save the world.

—Donna Fridrych

PART I

The World Situation

We Are World Citizens

Like it or not, we are world citizens. We live on the Earth, not Jupiter or another planet, and that means we are citizens of this planet. We could rightly call ourselves Earth Citizens. The Covid-19 pandemic and global warming shocked much of the world into acknowledging this reality.

In 2019, the failure to address rising global temperatures prompted many of our younger generation to ban together, march in the streets, and demand action from governments. But, not much changed. Then came Covid-19—the first pandemic we have seen since the Spanish flu in 1918. The virus quickly spread to every major country on the planet with dire consequences. Fear and panic escalated throughout the world. Unemployment soared as the world entered a global recession. Conspiracy theories flooded the Internet, and some countries began blaming each other for causing the pandemic.

But in addition to the threat of global warming and the Covid-19 pandemic, world citizens are vulnerable to a host of other dangers: mass shootings, terrorist attacks, cyber threats, financial meltdowns, racial injustices, biochemical warfare, identity theft, and thousands of refugees forced to flee their countries—a horrific list of tragedies that make the earth feel like an unsafe place to live.

Covid-19 may
be the final wake-up
call that Mother Earth
gives us.

She tried to warn us when Alaskan glaciers began melting a hundred times faster than scientists anticipated. We didn't listen. She tried to warn us again when massive fires in Australia destroyed 46 million acres, 5,900 buildings, and killed at least thirty-four people and one billion animals. But, again, we didn't listen.

It took Covid-19 to bring the world to a halt. The pandemic killed many of Mother Earth's children and, at least for a while, changed the behavior of many people on the planet. Suddenly the air on the planet became clearer because Her children stopped spewing toxic emissions by driving cars and flying in airplanes. The demand for oil plummeted to the lowest level in history, forcing some oil and gas companies into bankruptcy.

It would take a very smart mother to devise such a dramatic wake-up call. Mother Nature wants to save Her children and their earthly home. We now have the opportunity to change our ways. The door is open to new possibilities, particularly after getting a glimpse during the global lockdown of what cleaner air would look like on the earth.

Global warming and the coronavirus pose a threat to humanity that could continue to escalate for years to come unless coordinated, cohesive action is taken by governments and citizens around the world. What if the earth's atmosphere heats up even faster than scientists have predicted? What if a new virus or a mutation of the virus develops and spreads around the world even more quickly next time—perhaps with deadlier consequences than Covid-19?

Whether it's the threat of global warming, a nuclear warfare, biological weapons, or some other disease, we haven't made much progress as far as creating a safe and prosperous world for all.

There is one obvious solution to these multiple threats: We need to work together to save the planet and its people. But the question is, will we? Will we work together, or will we continue to undermine each other as we have in the past by building up our military defenses and competing with each other in a variety of destructive ways?

While there are a few extremely wealthy philanthropists on the planet, such as Oprah Winfrey, Bill and Melinda Gates, and Warren Buffet, who have made great strides in addressing poverty and disease, why haven't we made more progress? Why haven't more people stepped up? Many people seem to ignore the fact that we are living in an unjust and dangerous world. I explore how we got here and how we can create a safer, better world in the next chapters.

Mistrust and Massacres

Back in 1873, U.S. President Ulysses S. Grant predicted that at some future time, the nations of earth would agree on a form of congress whose representatives would make decisions as binding as the Supreme Court. He envisioned a time when armies and navies would no longer be necessary. Since then, we have seen two world wars and countless other wars between and within countries. It's hard to imagine our world without war. The world that President Grant envisioned seems like a utopian dream.

Rarely has there been a time in human history when some part of the world has not been at war.

Since earliest times, the impetus to fight has been fear of scarcity; tribal groups attacked each other to secure food and territory. Over time, various revolutions arose in the world as people battled not only for basic survival but human rights. Wars were waged in the name of God and religions. Many wars erupted as nations tried to expand their territory, influence, and take control of other countries.

Darwinism and Social Darwinism took hold in Europe before the First World War; the theories held that the struggle between nations and races is natural, and only the fittest nations are destined and deserve to survive. With that belief, it is easy to see how the two world wars began, and it explains how Germany justified the mass killing of Jews during World War II.

World War I left seventeen million people dead and twenty million wounded. In the decades before the war began in 1914, diplomatic clashes between Italy, France, Germany, Britain, Austria-Hungary, and Russia led to tension and misunderstanding. These six countries became polarized and formed alliances with countries with common aims and enemies. The friction escalated with the assassination of Archduke Franz Ferdinand of Austria, but the seeds of war had been planted long before that event.

World War II began in the West with the invasion

of Poland by Germany. Global war in the Pacific began after Japan, which sought to dominate Asia and the Pacific, launched a surprise attack on the United States and European colonies in the Pacific. The war lasted six years and killed approximately sixty million people. Of note is that far more civilians than military personnel lost their lives during World War II, many dying due to genocide, mass bombings, disease, and starvation.

World War II brought many technological advances in warfare, including the atomic bomb and the assault rifle. The world's first programmable computer developed by IBM was exploited to keep track of prisoners in Nazi prison camps.

Shortly after World War II, the Cold War between the Soviet Union and the United States and their respective allies began, which lasted for decades. With the struggle for dominance by world powers, it was a period of geopolitical tension. The Cold War finally ended in 1991 with the dissolution of the Soviet Union. Fortunately, we were spared the tragic carnage seen in the two world wars, most likely because of the nuclear threat both countries wielded. It is often said that the third world war will be the end of the planet.

Numbers can't begin to give a picture of the magnitude of the tragedies of war, because they don't include humanitarian crises, hyperinflation, injured and misplaced people, and high levels of starvation and disease. That said, the number of people who continue to be killed in wars is horrifying.

The world has seen sixty-three wars since World War II ended in 1945.

Four of these wars resulted in death tolls greater than one million, and four other wars each had death counts greater than three million. Today there are twenty wars in progress around the planet—in Asia, Africa, Latin America, and the Middle East—wars that are leading to millions of displaced people and humanitarian crises.

History tells us that before a war breaks out, there are warning signs evident in tension between or within nations. Since 2010, a renewed state of tension has occurred between the Soviet successor state Russia and the U.S. and its allies, along with growing tension between an increasingly powerful China and the U.S and its allies. Distrust between nations has escalated as a result.

During the Covid-19 pandemic,
rumors spread on the
social media accusing
both China and the U.S. of
intentionally creating the
virus in laboratories and
releasing it to the public.

China expelled thirteen journalists based in China from three U.S. newspapers, thereby intensifying the diplomatic feud between the two nations and impacting the flow of information.

The U.S. Secretary of State
accused China and Iran
of covering up
the Covid-19
outbreak in their nations;
some reporters claimed
that the latter accusation
moved Iran and the
U.S. closer to war.

This is a frightening thought since Iran has tried to develop nuclear weapons for years.

The U.S. accused the World Health Organization

(WHO) of siding with China, and withheld money that millions of people around the world depend upon. Italy accused Germany of withholding needed medical supplies. Other actions taken during the pandemic, such as the failure of the U.S. to remove tariffs on gloves and respirators from China, may have actually decreased the flow of vital medical supplies to the U.S. during the outbreak, and raised costs for the medical providers who were fighting the virus.

While negative rhetoric between governments intensified during the pandemic, much of the medical community shared information in a desperate attempt to find cures for the virus. A U.S. senator, who was one of three physicians in the Senate, praised China for doing an outstanding job of sharing information with the rest of the world. But unfortunately, positive statements such as this, which could have increased cooperation between the two superpowers, were infrequent and sometimes viewed with suspicion.

A Gallup poll in February 2020 found that American distrust of Beijing had increased from 57% to 67%.

In April 2020,
tensions between
China and the U.S. escalated
when three warships from
the U.S. Seventh Fleet
and an Australian
frigate sailed
into the disputed
South China Sea
in a show of force.

Also in 2020, the U.S. planned to make changes to all branches of its armed forces in order to better compete militarily with China and Russia.

The past decade has seen
an increase in violent
sectarian and religious
persecution in many countries.

The Middle East has Islamic extremists waging global jihad, as well as power struggles between Sunni and Shia Muslims. In Africa, violence between Christians and Muslims has escalated. North Korea has incarcerated Christians in harsh labor camps. There has also been a rise in Jewish hate crimes in several countries.

Recently we have seen a sharp increase in white nationalist and white supremacy movements, particularly in Germany, Austria, France, and the U.S.

The slogan "Make Germany Hate Again" (MGHA), printed on red hats, was reminiscent of hats worn in the 2016 American election. A group called the Identarians, who promote keeping immigrants out of Europe, has been indirectly linked to some of the mass shootings in Australia and Norway. A killing of a young girl in Charlottesville, Virginia, brought focus to the Neo-Nazi movement in the U.S. A shooting in El Paso, Texas, brought attention to the hatred of Mexican immigrants. In April 2020, the U.S. government designated a Russian white supremacist group, which has ties to U.S. and European white supremacist groups, as terrorists.

As large groups of immigrants seeking a better life flooded into Europe and the U.S., the rise of white nationalism was almost inevitable. White men have ruled the world for centuries, and their dominancy and way of life is being threatened. Given that mindset, it is natural that they would feel threatened, although it certainly does not justify hate crimes.

Racial injustice reached a boiling point in June of 2020, when a video capturing George Floyd, an African American, being tortured and murdered by a police officer in Minneapolis was released by the bystander who shared the horrifying scene on social media. Demonstrations, riots, and looting not witnessed in the U.S. since the 1960s erupted not only in America but in many cities around the world.

The Internet has served as a positive tool for connecting people in the world and calling global attention to social injustice. Yet it has also been a vehicle for "hate" groups, and resulted in the spread of misinformation, rumors, and mistrust in governments. Mistrust often leads to hate, and hate often leads to war. If we could look at the world from another planet's perspective, the cycle of mistrust, hate, escalating violence, human indignities, and warfare would seem endless.

So here we are … a planet upon which the blood of millions has been shed. Some estimates say up to 1.5 billion people could have been killed since the beginning of human existence. In addition to military battles, food shortages have killed many innocent people. Rape, torture, and other atrocities have occurred in many countries in war times.

Given this summary of global conflicts, it's easy to see why mistrust has grown over time between nations and between groups within nations. What rational person could look at the atrocities that have occurred in recent history and not be suspicious about the motives of another country? It's not surprising that some people think the U.S. would do anything to maintain its number-one superpower status, including creating Covid-19 in a secret lab in China. It's understandable that some people would suspect China, not the U.S., initiated Covid-19 and didn't accurately report its spread. Governments themselves fuel the fire of blame and mistrust with rhetoric that's often untrue or misleading at best. It is extremely difficult for the average person in any country to differentiate between propaganda and truth.

As history tells us, there
were rising tensions and
conflicts long before the
two world wars.
No one knows whether
we have reached the
level of tension that could
ignite another world war.

It's impossible to say what kind of events might spark such a tragedy. What I do know is that the drums of warmongers are beating in many parts of the world. The sound is palpable. The rhetoric is escalating.

PART II

Leading the Change

Eliminating a
Patriarchal Mindset

Warlike mentality is evident throughout the fabric of our global society.

Domination, being on top, beating the other guy, maintaining power over others ... this is the mindset we have seen in our leaders throughout history. This is the mindset of patriarchal leadership.

The world has been a patriarchal society for over five thousand years—a society in which men largely hold the power and women are largely excluded from it. Men wield power no matter where you look. The leaders of a patriarchal society typically demonstrate qualities associated with masculine behavior: rational thinking, aggressiveness, strength, need for control, and competitiveness.

In the early days, killing other humans for food and protecting oneself from attack was necessary to survive. Kill versus be killed became embedded in the human DNA. During the hunter-gatherer times, men excelled at protecting their turf and providing for themselves and their families. Fast forward ten thousand years, men provided for their families by operating small farms and engaging in trade for a living.

With the industrial revolution, we saw the growth of large corporations with global intent. By the 1890s, the world saw the development of many corporations still in existence today—steel, oil, shipping, and chemical companies. Men led these global corporations that manufactured products and conveniences and enhanced the lives of many in the developed world—electricity, automobiles, food security, medicine, and technological innovations. Though corporations have contributed much good to the world and have made our lives easier, they have also caused some of the serious challenges we face today, such as the air pollution that has led to global warming.

Although women in recent decades have made

significant inroads in the work force, approximately

> 90% of the world's largest
> companies are led by men,
> and men lead most nations,
> especially those with economic
> power and influence.

Male domination is particularly striking in the number one superpower in the world, the U.S., where no woman has ever been elected president and men hold 95% of Fortune 500 CEO positions.

Since my views on patriarchal society are based on my personal experience, a bit of my background seems warranted here. In the seventies, I was hired as one of the first women into the consulting division of a Big 8 accounting firm. I worked almost exclusively with men in Fortune 500 companies and learned what was necessary to get ahead in the corporate world. And I was quite successful for a woman of my era, eventually becoming acting Chief Information Officer (CIO) for United Airlines, and later, interim CEO of the United Airlines Employees' Credit Union, the sixth largest credit union in the U.S. at the time.

During my career, the reigning style of corporate

management was authoritarian and dogmatic. Today this is still the predominant style in most companies and governments. Leaders often attempt to project an image of power. Although some men come across as nonaggressive, underneath that veneer can be someone with steely-eyed callousness reflected in their decisions.

Although I enjoyed working with men, I didn't have a lot of respect for many of my male bosses. While some of them demonstrated domineering behavior before they were promoted, others didn't become combative and ruthless until after assuming power. Perhaps they thought such behavior was expected of them.

Looking beneath their external behavior, however,

I think we'd see many men in high positions feel insecure.

Some reach leadership positions without having the necessary background and experience to handle their new job. Some become overwhelmed by their position, which may cause them to act tough and be bullies.

The extent of the bullying behavior they exhibit often depends on their level of insecurity.

Although I had bosses and saw some men in authority who contradicted this behavior, they were the exception. Humility was an undervalued attribute, and arrogance was often in full display.

Women who reach executive positions usually have to work harder than their male counterparts to get promoted, and, perhaps as a result, they do not feel as insecure. They don't feel the need to strut around and pound their chest.

A frequent tactic used by the patriarchy is cronyism —the practice of promoting friends and family regardless of their qualifications.

Cronyism is often why incompetent men get ahead in business and politics, and also explains why women hold fewer top positions.

Equally damaging is the practice of discrediting foes. During my career I repeatedly saw powerful technology companies systematically destroy the reputation of those who did not support or promote their products. I became a target for such abuse on multiple occasions. I remember standing back and thinking to myself that working in a corporate environment was just another kind of warfare … a war in which only the fittest survive.

Reaching top levels in a corporation or government usually depends upon beating your internal and external competitors.

A warlike mentality is useful for getting ahead.

Many executives feel that the survival of their company and their employees depends upon them, which is often the case. The same mentality applies to government leadership. Perhaps memories buried deep within men's DNA get triggered, and that old survival instinct kicks in.

While some people maintain that power corrupts, a study published in 2012 in the *Journal of Applied Psychology* found that power doesn't really corrupt; rather, it only heightens pre-existing ethical tendencies. This study supports my experiences. Power can either increase a person's tendency toward moral behavior or increase their tendency toward unethical behavior.

Destructive behavior by corporations is actually supported by U.S. law.

The law mandates that U.S. corporations, as legal institutions, must relentlessly pursue profitability without exception—in spite of any potential harm done to others or to the planet. This law has resulted in huge fines being given to corporations, because they are legally bound to make decisions that generate the most money for their company, rather than doing the "right" thing for people and the planet. Although there has recently been some interest expressed in pushing companies to improve upon environmental, social, and governance (ESG) practices, little progress has been made. This does not bode well for global warming.

Although fines levied to corporations can amount to millions of dollars, the levies are miniscule in terms of a company's net worth. Making harmful decisions is far more profitable for the company than doing the right thing.

Usually the top decision makers don't go to jail because they are protected by the law that dictates they make the most profitable decision for their company. Unless there is a public outcry, the fine is paid and the consequences, such as the pollution of air and water, show up in the environment.

I also find advertising disingenuous that promotes a corporation as being a caring, global citizen. Such advertising is often bullshit, because most executives will just make the most profitable decision for their company. Needless to say, many companies outside of the U.S. will make similar or even more harmful decisions in order to remain competitive.

Given where we are today, I do not understand how anyone could think that a continuation of patriarchal leadership will lead us to peace and prosperity. While a bow and arrow might have been the weapon of choice in days gone by, the atomic bomb, biochemical agents, and destructive corporate practices are among the arsenal of weapons men use to dominate the world today. I see no evidence that this patriarchal mindset is changing.

The superpowers
are augmenting their
militaries and ratcheting
up combative rhetoric
and actions.

The chest-thumping we hear in the news today would be ludicrous, if we weren't facing so many real dangers. Rather than improving, world tensions seem to be getting worse, especially since the Covid-19 pandemic, when one would think cooperation and teamwork would be paramount.

Five thousand
years of war
and conflict
is enough!

It is time for leadership to put down its guns. It is time for corporate greed at the expense of the environment and human justice to stop. It is time for a new kind of leadership. It is time for a new mindset.

It is time for
a new skill set to
lead the world.

Why Women Must Lead

It's been a hard climb for women to rise to leadership positions in our patriarchal society. In many ways the progress women have made in attaining top positions, particularly in government, is remarkable. Since 1950, women have been elected or appointed by a governing committee or parliament in 87 countries to be heads of state or government. Included in that count is women who have had acting titles. Not included in that count is women who have been members of a collective head of state and monarchs. Even though some of the female heads of state were in charge for a very short time, and others were given acting titles, a map showing all the countries that have been led by women since 1950 reflects roughly half of the physical territory in the world. However, what also stands out in large parts of the world, such as major areas of Africa, as well as Mexico, the Soviet Union, and the U.S., is that these countries have not had at least one woman as their top leader. The Soviet Union has at least had female members in collective head-of-state bodies. While Mexico and the U.S. have never had a female president, Hillary Clinton did win the popular vote in the U.S. presidential election in 2016.

Perhaps one of the best examples of what often happens to women is the case of Soong Ching-ling of China, who was acting co-chairperson of China for over three years, and later the acting head of state. It wasn't until her final illness (and two weeks before her death) that she was given the special title of "Honorary President of the People's Republic of China" without an "acting" qualifier.

By the end of 2019, there were only 29 female heads of government. A map of the world now shows only a small amount of territory being led by women.

It appears women made significant progress in attaining government leadership in the world during the twentieth century, but then lost much of their influence during the twenty-first century.

Although one could conjecture as to the reasons for the loss of power, the fact is that most of the world has returned to being ruled by the patriarchy. In addition, with the exception of Germany, most of the countries led by women today do not account for much of the economic power in the world.

Another observation worth mentioning is that when a particular area in the world, such as Latin America or the Scandinavian countries, has had at least one female leader, there is a higher likelihood that other countries within that area or continent will have elected female leaders. For the most part, only a few of the female leaders, such as Margaret Thatcher of the United Kingdom and Andrea Merkel of Germany, have received worldwide recognition for their leadership.

The patriarchy is also clearly in charge of big business. Although I have found inconsistencies in studies reporting the percentage of female CEOs worldwide, most conclude that the number is less than 10%. Most studies also show the Asian Pacific countries as having a significantly higher percentage of female CEOs than in the U.S. or Europe, with the U.S. consistently reporting women as leading only 5% of Fortune 500 companies. Prior to doing business in many countries in the world, I thought the U.S. was ahead of other countries in promoting women to leadership positions. I found this to be a false assumption.

Many women have also been influential in secondary positions in government and business. There is a big difference, however, between having the top position and being number two or holding a C-suite executive position.

Although women started making progress in their business careers during the 1980s, many continued to work in low-paying jobs and had little chance of getting ahead in the corporate world. Men often promoted each other to the exclusion of women (cronyism), women's skills were not as valued as men's skills, and women often worked in administrative or supportive fields—organizations that were not viewed as being operationally critical for their companies and that did not prepare them for top leadership roles. My book, *Reflections from the Glass Ceiling*, explores in detail why women haven't made more progress.

One reason for women's lack of advancement is management style. I was not alone in being told my style was too inclusive and people-oriented. Some women who did reach higher levels in management mimicked the male model by acting dogmatic, superior, and exclusive. Yet, I did see some exceptions, cases where women chose to manage according to a more inclusive style, and their intuition and ability to multi-task and foster teamwork produced spectacular results. Unfortunately, most women were shamed into repressing their natural talents.

Studies since the late 1800s have attempted to prove the inferiority of female brains. One study (recently supported by a Harvard professor) found the female brain to be different than the male brain in nineteen distinct ways, including weighing less—inferring that the weight difference meant women were less intelligent than men.

The fact is that all humans are born with two hemispheres in their brain—a left and right hemisphere, often referred to as the left brain and right brain. Each hemisphere tends to preside over different functions and excels at solving different kinds of problems.

The left brain, or left hemisphere, is associated with logic, thinking, reasoning, order, control, and identifying with the individual; it characterizes being male. The right brain, or right hemisphere, is associated with creativity, emotion, relationships, putting things together, identifying with the group, and holistic thinking; it characterizes being female, and is more fluid and flexible than male-dominated thinking. Traditionally, men have been praised and rewarded for acting with their logic-oriented, unemotional left brain, and women have been denigrated for operating from their right brain and acting too emotional.

Some people are born with a balance of both the right and left hemispheres. Though many people exhibit left-brain or right-brain dominance, that dominance can be changed or balanced with training and experience. Societal influence can also change a person's natural disposition: boys are sometimes taught that it is unmanly to be compassionate, and girls may be taught that boys don't like girls who are smart.

In 2017, Google fired an engineer who wrote

a memo claiming that the low number of women in technical positions was due to biologic (brain) differences. This was a watershed moment for women, because even though this engineer had the audacity to write the memo, his thinking brought to light what many believed in the field of technology. While it may be true that there are fewer women in the technological industries, this is primarily because they have not been trained in left-brain disciplines.

I suspect there are many more women who have either left-brain dominance or balanced hemispheres than we know of, because society expects women to be right-brained, just as it expects men to be left-brained. We merely need to look at women of note in history to confirm that bias.

Women are just as capable as men of left-brain thinking.

The problem is not due to lack of ability, but lack of recognition of their achievements.

One example of unsung recognition was Eunice Newton Foote, an American scientist, inventor, and women's rights campaigner in the 1800s. Credit for her work went unnoticed until 2010 when a retired geologist found a paper of hers published in 1857 and realized that she was the first person to make the connection between carbon dioxide and climate change. Over a hundred years after her death, Foote was recognized in 2019 for her groundbreaking findings on the greenhouse effect (i.e. global warming).

Another undervalued woman of science and invention was Hedy Lamarr, a well-known movie actress during the 1930s and 40s. In addition to her gorgeous appearance, Lamar had an inventive mind. She and co-inventor George Antheil came up with a new communication system that was intended to guide torpedoes to their targets during World War II. Although not used during the war, the invention is the basis for today's WiFi, GPS, and Bluetooth communication systems. Lamarr received several awards in her later years after her patent expired, and in 2014, she was inducted into the National Inventors Hall of Fame (four years after her death).

Katherine Johnson was another phenomenal

woman of science. As an African American woman born in 1918, Johnson had to battle both racism and sexism to pursue her profession as a mathematician. Working at NASA, her calculations of orbital mechanics were critical to the success of the first manned spaceflights, and earned her the Presidential Medal of Freedom and a Congressional Gold Medal. Recent documentary films have credited both Johnson's and Lamarr's contributions to society.

Some men who have been raised with a patriarchal mindset don't care to give such women credit. It's as if they feel shamed by being outsmarted by a woman, and to give them credit would take away from their manhood. Fortunately, there are men who have stepped forward and insisted that women receive the recognition that they deserve for their work.

During my career, I was frequently praised for my ability to handle personnel and human resource issues. I remember attending a class in my early career in which multiple-choice testing was administered in order to reveal a person's inherent management style. As was often the case, I was the only female in the class. While most of my male colleagues received results that were in keeping with the management style in vogue at the time (a domineering, dogmatic, dictatorial style), my style was deemed too inclusive. Since my skills were viewed as female-oriented (and therefore not essential), I was pigeonholed into secondary, supportive functions.

As I pursued jobs in fields known for left-brain expertise, I was rarely given just due in terms of title or compensation. I would like to have been recognized and compensated accordingly for the many large projects I led, because I was really good at designing computer systems. With only an acting CIO title, I did a remarkable job of keeping a major airline's computer systems running efficiently for over a year during a time when the company was in turmoil and in the midst of changing top management. I would like to have received more recognition for championing and leading the first implementation of E-Ticket software, which changed the way ticketing was done in the airline industry; I sold the software to thirteen other airlines for millions of dollars, and it was entered into the Smithsonian's Permanent Research Collection. My collaborative skills, so often dismissed as inconsequential, enabled me to work with many contentious departments in multiple companies, and to lead a team that worked with the FBI after 9/11 to gather critical data around the clock. One of the accomplishments I am most proud of is that while serving as interim CEO, I protected thousands of employees' hard-earned money by quickly diversifying a company that had never attempted diversification. While I know in my heart that I wouldn't have been given responsibility to lead these important efforts without having the necessary skills, I had to be content with acting and interim titles, and small increases in pay. To state this list of accomplishments may seem like bragging, something men do frequently without a second thought. Women need to take credit for their accomplishments in order to be recognized and considered for promotions.

Most women, as well as
many male and female minorities,
will be overlooked and undervalued
at some point in their careers.

Many readers will be able to identify with the anger and frustration I felt during my own career. My point, however, is not to vent anger about women's unjust treatment. The purpose of this book is to show why women must be put in charge.

I know it's difficult to put aside the hurts and slights of the past, but women must do so in order to save the world.

While anger can be motivating, indulging in it only adds to the toxicity of the planet; it doesn't help move us forward.

My personal experience managing thousands of employees supports the idea that it is the right-brain, feminine skills which are desperately needed today. Before the age of computers, having solid left-brain skills was imperative, especially the ability to gather and analyze a lot of information. Now, with technology and information at our fingertips, it is easy to feed data into a computer and come out with logic-based results. It is the added dimension of empathy and intuition that the computer and artificial intelligence (AI) lacks and programmers have failed to emulate. The computer also cannot easily replicate the results from human teamwork and collaboration, where one person builds on the idea of another with unforeseen, spectacular results.

Because computer technology can replicate many of the left-brain skills, it is the right-brain skills that are critically needed in leadership roles today. Collaboration, intuition, creativity, multi-tasking, compassion, teamwork, sophisticated interpersonal skills, and the ability to influence others and to interpret feelings, ideas, and facts are strengths that many women possess.

These skills have not been highly valued by the patriarchy, although some grudgingly admit that they can produce amazing results.

Women tend to consider more factors than men when making decisions; they tend to think globally and holistically. Imaging studies have shown that a man's brain shuts down when he has to rely on more than three or four factors; the elevated stress hormones diminish his focus.

One of my bosses during my career surprised

me by saying that he would promote a woman over a man for a management position. I was especially surprised because he surpassed anyone I knew for bullying and yelling. He became so angry at times that I think he lost touch with himself. One time, after I had upset him by challenging his decision, I ran out of his office as fast as I could, with him running close behind me, and hurried into the ladies' room. That's why I was shocked when he promoted me and said he would take a competent woman anytime over a man for a leadership position.

I also remember a point in my career when I had two thousand technical employees reporting to me—men and women from every race. Two women stood out at the time, and still do today. Both women were hard-working, and had average technical experience. Though other employees may have been more advanced technically, both women had developed solid left-brain skills. But their right-brain skills, especially their intuition, were extraordinary. They seemed to effortlessly assimilate facts and come up with new ideas that were both practical and inspiring. Their ability to communicate and motivate teams of people to implement their ideas was equally awesome. Most notably, intelligent men in high-level positions seemed eager to hear their every insight. And yet these two women were never given their just dues in terms of position and pay. These are the kind of women that we need to lead the world today. Solid, logic-oriented, left-brain skills, along with collaborative, right-brain skills are needed in both government and business.

Because of their balanced skills, female CEOs at some of the biggest Chinese and U.S. firms are earning higher pay than many men. There are reasons that women such as Li Qingping of CITIC Bank, Dong Mingzhu of Gree Electric Appliances, Mary Barra of GM, and Ginni Rometty of IBM have been paid such huge salaries. There are reasons that Andrea Merkel, a scientist and the first female Chancellor of Germany, is seen in photos with the other male leaders in the European Union (EU) looking to her for direction. Although some have been critical of her, particularly of her immigration policies, she has served four terms, is recognized as the de facto leader of the EU, has steered Germany through financial crisis and return to growth—and most famously, stood up to the American President after he made racist comments against four Democratic congresswomen. All of these women were highly skilled in left-brain disciplines, and used their right-brain talents to lead.

Given the distinct difference in management style between the patriarchal mindset currently leading many businesses and governments and a feminine model of collaboration and inclusivity, it is clear in my mind which style of future leadership we need in our world. Another thing to consider is that in the number one superpower country in the world, women are well positioned to lead: Women in the U.S. now control half of the personal wealth, receive half of advanced degrees, and often increase the bottom line when they lead corporations. Worldwide women control about thirty percent of personal wealth.

It's time for a major change in global leadership. I don't understand why anyone would think that continued patriarchal leadership will change the world for the better. How could anyone possibly think that physical strength and combative rhetoric are going to protect us from nuclear bombs, chemical warfare, biological agents, global warming, and other dangers? Likewise, I don't understand why anyone wouldn't think that female leadership stands a better chance of creating a better world. Isn't having two highly skilled hemispheres in the brain better than having only one? Isn't it obvious that collaborative, inclusive skills will lead to better results for all? Perhaps that's really the issue: current leadership does not want to achieve better results for all of mankind.

Being compassionate doesn't mean women can't or won't make difficult decisions. Women often demonstrate extraordinary strength when faced with adversity and hard choices.

On the other hand, many men shrink from confrontation and emotional issues.

Promoting women rather than men to leadership positions today is not a matter of gender preference. It is a matter of who has the skills for the job at hand—to create a better world.

The goal should be to change the patriarchal mindset that has been leading the world for centuries by replacing it with government and business leadership that will create a prosperous and safe environment for everyone.

Just as women needed to develop their left-brain skills in the last century, men need to develop their right-brain skills now. I believe they can do this over time, but only if they want to change and don't see "feminine" attributes as threatening to their manhood. In the meantime, women must lead the way in creating a safer, more nurturing world. The world needs women and men from all countries collaborating and working together. We do not need more bombs and weapons of mass destruction. We do not need more corporations damaging the environment.

In order to create a safe
and prosperous world,
women must lead corporations and
governments worldwide—particularly
those corporations and governments
that have major economic
influence and power.

Women must lead as CEOs of companies and presidents of countries. Instead of men leading 90% of large corporations worldwide, women need to lead corporations by a similar percentage—until the time comes when we have succeeded in creating a better world. Women need to assume the top positions in government, rather than having men lead the superpower nations and influential countries in the world.

Let me be clear … I am saying that women should lead by becoming the presidents of China, Russia, and the U.S., as well as other countries in the world.

It's been "a man's world" for a long time. Let's see if living in a world led by women can lead to a more just and less threatening world.

PART III

What It Will Take to Become a Global Family

The Foundation

The challenges that women will face in leading the world are significant. But there are some viable solutions for addressing these challenges if world citizens adopt the proper mindset.

Much as we talk about globalization, that doesn't mean we are acting like global citizens.

Globalization simply means that the national economies of the planet are highly integrated through trade, investment, capital flow, labor migration, and technology. Goods and people move among different countries. Today the world is so interconnected that a recession in one major country often causes a global recession. Although globalization may be viewed negatively by some, the probability of the world's countries returning to a state of total protectionism is very low.

Covid-19 has forced us to reconsider what it means to act globally. Although some countries may be tempted to shut down their borders, it's difficult to imagine the world going back to isolation for long. Since 2014, China has spent almost one trillion dollars in Latin America, Africa, the Middle East, and Asia. Tourism before Covid-19 was a booming industry across the world with a value of more than nine trillion dollars. The U.S. has also invested heavily in foreign securities. If the U.S. were to close its borders and shut down immigration entirely, the country would lose what has made it great, and what has enabled it to become the number one superpower in the world. There is hardly an invention or company in most U.S. industries that has not been led by an immigrant.

I can't imagine us all going back to a time when we didn't travel to other countries, buy goods and services from other countries, and marry and enjoy relationships with people from other countries. That said, what are the chances that people from all over the world will begin to think of themselves as part of a global family, and act accordingly? I would say that with the current patriarchal mindset the probability of such a change is almost nil. Without a radical change in mindset, particularly by the superpower nations, we stand a better chance of starting a new civilization on Mars.

The earth has never had a global government, although some people in history have envisioned and promoted the concept. The closest the world has come to having a global government is the United Nations, which was established in 1945 after World War II. It is primarily an advisory organization with the stated purpose of promoting cooperation between national governments, rather than exerting power over them. Although the United Nations Security Council has the ability to issue mandatory resolutions, it has had limited effect.

In 1954 the World Service Authority (WSA) was founded as a non-profit organization with the intent of promoting world citizenship, world law, and world government. Although the WSA has had offices in New York City, Basel, London, and Tokyo, the organization has gained little traction thus far.

The WHO was established to direct international health within the United Nations and to lead in global health responses. As mentioned previously, it has come under attack from the U.S. and other countries for its handling of the Covid-19 pandemic.

Consider what an Earth Family would look like if the human race were to decide to live and work harmoniously together for the peace, prosperity, and safety of all world citizens.

> Being an Earth Family could mean thinking of every person in the world as part of your own family.

People of a family usually do not want to kill each other; with a new mindset, we could do away with systems of deterrent. The leaders of an Earth Family would make sure that all its citizens have food and shelter. An Earth Family would work together to protect its family from disease, famine, or harm. It would want to make sure that each member of the family has the chance to feel happy and fulfilled. Values such as service for others would be highly valued in an Earth Family.

Countries that see their children starving would embrace the concept of an Earth Family. People who have had to flee their countries because of violence, religious persecution, and famine would welcome a change that would assure them a safe place to live. Those countries that see no future for their citizens, other than more poverty, illness, and war, would welcome such a change.

Assume, for a moment, that all the citizens of the world want to become an Earth Family. Described below are some stipulations that could lay the foundation for the creation of such a world. While some of the stipulations may seem more difficult to achieve than others, all nations would be allowed to maintain their individual cultures, customs, and religions. Although a great many details would need to be worked out, a minimal level of consensus or compromise could most likely be reached on items 1 through 7, but only if there is a prevailing intention that everyone wants to establish a true Earth Family.

1. All nations would agree on universal forms of governance.

Although forms of government such as communism, democracy, and dictatorship seem diametrically opposed, perhaps the world could agree that in certain situations some forms of government work better for the people of a country or nation than others. For example, the extreme lockdown measures that the People's Republic of China exerted over its citizens in 2020 with a communist form of government may have prevented the Covid-19 epidemic from becoming even worse. Although initially slow to act, once the virus was recognized, China's government was able to quickly shut down certain areas of the country and mobilize its reaction to the crisis. On the other hand, South Korea is an example of a democratic form of government that was able to pretty successfully manage the virus. America's capitalistic culture with the aid of large pharmaceutical companies may have been able to expedite cures for the virus.

Some argue that America, generally considered the best example of democracy in the world, has an oligarchic form of government in which a smattering of individuals with a lot of money and some big corporations with 12,000 lobbyists exercise an inordinate influence. Even the two political parties in the U.S. seem to lean toward different forms of government; while the Democrats lean toward a socialist model, the Republicans lean toward a conservative form.

Given the prejudicial, negative bias that many people hold about various forms of government, instead of attempting to immediately reach total agreement on a universal form of government, world citizens might agree to some umbrella form of governance that would allow for individual politics. Or someone may envision an entirely new system based on past governing experiences that everyone could embrace.

2. New laws and governance would be established for businesses and corporations.

Educating the world about the harm being done to the planet by governments and businesses is fundamental to addressing this issue. Once understood, laws and rules could be easily established that would eliminate or drastically reduce destructive behavior to the planet, and that would promote environmental, social, and governance practices.

3. All weapons of mass destruction of any kind would be abolished, and all defense budgets would be eliminated or significantly reduced.

Many countries are currently trying to prohibit the proliferation of nuclear weapons. The Iran nuclear deal of 2015 was an attempt by several nations to prevent Iran from developing nuclear weapons. Unfortunately, the effort seemed to be successful until the U.S. withdrew its support in 2018. If the world's citizens changed their mindset, however, such that an Earth Family was committed not to annihilate the planet, a concerted effort to eliminate and prevent the use of any nuclear weapons might be achievable.

In addition, if all countries would agree to significantly reduce or eliminate their defense spending, close to two trillion dollars could be saved annually.

I realize this would be a frightening prospect for many, particularly leaders in the superpower nations who are in fact increasing their military spending. Perhaps an incremental decrease in defense spending could be put into effect until trust between nations is established. I hearken back to the words of President Grant who said that at some future time armies and navies would no longer be necessary.

Just imagine all the good that two trillion dollars could do for the world.
That's ten trillion dollars over five years.

4. All countries would agree to free trade.

Although there are many trade agreements that could be expanded upon, none would be necessary if everyone could agree upon a bartering system, or a universal system that provides all world citizens with fair, sustainable compensation for goods and services performed.

5. All countries would freely share information and technologies in order to keep the planet safe from disease and other harm.

Most countries would agree that after the devastating experience of Covid-19, the WHO needs to be strengthened, or some other means should be found to prevent another pandemic. There could be many benefits from establishing healthcare as a global industry. We already see many healthcare professionals working together and sharing research and information.

> The healthcare industry could lead the way in establishing a cooperative model for other industries.

6. All citizens would be provided basic food and shelter, no matter where they lived.

In spite of the increase in the world's population, great progress has been made in decreasing poverty. As of 2015 (the most recent actual poverty data available), 10% of the world's population lived on less than U.S. $1.90 a day, which is the commonly accepted barometer for poverty. Although that percentage is deplorable given all the resources in the world, it's encouraging to see that this shows a decrease of 36% since 1990. While there are still significant areas of poverty (with half of the extreme poor living in Sub-Saharan Africa), it is a wonderful example of what the world can do when it works together. This is an area where a small reduction in defense spending could go a long way.

The earth has all the resources
it needs to feed and shelter
every person on earth,
and enable the fulfilment of
all humans, animals, and plant life.

7. Russia would give up its quest for territorial expansion.

With the dissolution of the Soviet Union in 1991, the successor state Russia lost its superpower status. Many historians see Russia's recent annexation of Crimea and the war with Ukraine as evidence that Russia wants to return to its superpower status by expanding its territory. Through its oil-rich and military influence, Russia has also recently gained power and influence in many areas of the Middle East. While it seems unlikely that Russia would willingly relinquish its quest for territorial expansion and influence, many countries are already trying to keep Russia's takeover attempts in check, and they might be successful if all other countries joined together to limit the country's maneuvering.

8. The superpower countries of China and the U.S. would relinquish their drive to maintain superiority over other nations.

This last stipulation will be the most difficult to achieve. Clear evidence of both countries' desire to retain their superpower status is reflected in the military buildup and economic investments we see today.

Many of China's citizens have been freed from poverty over the past four decades and lead a middle-class life. In the meantime, the Chinese government has increased its influence around the world. In addition to investing heavily in its military forces, China has invested in infrastructure and other projects in foreign countries. Like it or not, much of the world is dependent on China, and it would cause decades of hardship were other countries to remove that dependency.

During my business dealings with many countries, China seemed superior to other countries as far as making smart, profitable business decisions that would pay off in the long term. We now see evidence of those long-term decisions in technological advances.

Most American companies, on the other hand, almost always take a short-term view when making decisions. What matters most to American executives is boosting the bottom line and increasing their company's stock price as quickly as possible; whereas Chinese companies make business decisions that pay off over time. It's hard to imagine most American executives using that kind of strategy. Although American corporations have been able to maintain much of their superiority to date, I worry about the ramifications of short-sighted decisions in the future.

So the question remains: why would China want to give up its superpower status? It is more likely that China, after years of making long-term investments, wants to become the number one superpower in the world.

The U.S. has long been seen as a beacon of light and hope for the world; it has been the leader in providing humanitarian aid to the world. It is also still seen as the most powerful nation in the world. Much of the U.S.'s superpower status is based on its strong economy, although the long-term effects of Covid-19 remain to be seen.

The idea that the U.S. is the greatest country on earth is often followed by saying it is the richest country in the world. With the U.S. controlling thirty percent of the world's wealth, it is difficult to understand why in the richest country in the world, forty percent of the population could not financially weather a small emergency. With so many Americans financially insecure, it is easy to understand why one of the U.S. presidential candidates in 2020, a self-declared democratic socialist, gained so much traction. Other factors, such as lower mortality rates and educational ranking also seem difficult to understand in the richest country in the world.

I wonder how U.S. citizens would feel if their country were no longer the "number one" superpower. What if the U.S. were no longer the business leader in the world because of the short-sighted greed of its business leaders over the past decades? What if other countries started demanding repayment for the billions of dollars in loans given to the U.S.? What if cyber threats were to become real and bring the economy to a halt? What if global warming reaches a point such that it cannot be reversed? I challenge anyone to deny that these possibilities are real. The U.S. may lose its number one superpower status, even if it is not ready to agree to stipulation number eight and relinquish its drive to maintain superiority.

Consider the alternative. If nothing changes in the world, China will see more protests and challenges to its authority. The U.S. will eventually lose its superiority, as it falls under its national debt and inferior education and healthcare systems. Russia will continue to try to expand its dominance in the world, and the Middle East will continue to have wars. Perhaps the world will continue to exist with all the threats that we see today … or, it may not continue to exist at all.

To take the leadership role from a patriarchy that has led the world for thousands of years will be challenging. But it may not be as difficult as many would think. Recently, there have been signs of unrest and resistance to the status quo in China and the U.S. In 2019-2020, Hong Kong saw ongoing protests over a bill that many saw as undermining its authority and civil liberties. Taiwan continues to resist China's attempts to bring its governance under China's rule. During the same time period, the U.S. saw demonstrations over racial injustice and global warming. These demonstrations and protests are signs of discontent within the two superpowers.

With the unrest we've seen
in many parts of the world,
this might be the perfect opportunity
for new worldwide leadership.

Recent events may be the
catalysts to propel
women to power.

Changing Our Prejudices and Biases

Women leaders will only be successful in transforming our world into a global family if everyone does their part—both women and men. We are all in this together, part of one world, connected beyond differences of race, nationality, or gender. The survival of the planet depends upon each of us thinking of ourselves as a member of an Earth Family. Call it the golden rule or the fundamental principle found at the heart of most religions, we must think of each other in a loving, peaceful way. We each need to do our part by opening our minds and exploring new ways of thinking, and thereby create a more loving and peaceful world. The main thing is to not hate people or ways different than our own, and to be wary of those who promote hatred. Each of us must examine our beliefs and assumptions, including people we know little about.

Although I blame patriarchal leadership for the critical state of the world today, most world citizens, including me, need to share in the blame.

Knowingly or unknowingly, most of us have contributed to global injustice by our prejudices and biases that have led to hatred of others.

We spew toxic energy into the atmosphere with our hateful thoughts and words, and don't realize the harm that we are doing to ourselves and others. Thoughts are energy, and energy cannot be destroyed.

Often our leaders are just a reflection of who we are and how we feel. The only way we will eliminate war and achieve peace is if each and every one of us looks into our minds and hearts to see what needs changing. That takes a willingness to be honest with ourselves, and to be open to the possibility that our prejudices and biases are inaccurate, sometimes based on false beliefs and assumptions.

Prejudices. We all have them. No one is immune to having them. Some come from our parents, teachers, and peers. Some come from the news, Internet, or television. Many come from our government spokespeople. Most prejudices involve thoughts about race, religion, and gender. Many prejudices are based on facts, while others are simply based on suspicion.

Prejudices and biases are often the reason that we don't trust those living in other nations or even people in our own country. They prevent us from working better together.

It is hard to imagine, let alone create, a safe, supportive world when we attribute evil intent to people in our own country or in other countries.

While there may be valid reasons to not trust some people, in many cases our prejudices are based on outdated, false, or incomplete information or propaganda.

Many of my own prejudices have proven to be false. My experiences doing business in many countries, in addition to having a multi-national family, have given me the opportunity to reflect on my own prejudices. I also had the opportunity to get a glimpse of the prejudices that some people have about Americans when I lived in France for a year and traveled throughout Europe.

What I found in doing business in Australia, Britain, Canada, China, Europe, Israel, Japan, Mexico, Singapore, and South America is that people from all over the world are much the same. We have the same desire to support and protect our families, to stay healthy, and to enjoy the pleasures in life. We have the same fears as well. Often I feel as comfortable with people from other nations as I do with my fellow countrymen.

What I also found is that most people in developed nations—with the exception of Americans—have an in-depth understanding of what's happening in countries around the world in addition to their own country. This often led me to believe that Americans were not as well-educated as people from other countries. Today China spends more money than the U.S. on translating and printing news about American culture and politics, although some of the translations may be meant for the purpose of disseminating propaganda. While in the past some of the world news has been to discredit adversaries, we should all demand that our government and news people provide objective coverage of global cultures and events. Such factual knowledge could help us to better know the members of our global family.

Beliefs matter because they determine how we view life, what actions we take or don't take, who we vote for, and how we think about and treat others in our own and other countries. While most people develop prejudices during their formative years, some maintain those biases throughout their lifetime.

Most people grow and change their capabilities and behaviors throughout their lifetime. They acquire education, training, and new experiences.

The problem arises when we don't allow people to evolve and change, when we rely on old or inaccurate thinking about them.

Unless we have firsthand, up-to-date experience or are certain about the credibility of the source of our beliefs, it is foolhardy to rely on secondhand information that may be tainted or intended for the purpose of brainwashing. Even most of our trusted teachers have biases.

Most important, when we accept others for who they are, the world changes. If we are going to develop an Earth Family, each of us must evaluate our prejudices and biases. The list of potential subjects for prejudice and bias is long. For example, as an American, how do you feel about communism and the leaders of a communistic regime? As a Chinese person, how do you feel about a capitalistic form of government and the wealth inequality in America?

As a man, do you think women are inherently weaker and less intelligent than men? Do you think female leadership would make your country more vulnerable to war?

As a heterosexual man or women, what do you think about gay men and women? Should they have all the same legal rights that you have? Should they be able to marry and raise children?

As a Protestant or Catholic, how do you feel about Islam? Are you concerned about terrorism linked to Muslim communities?

All our biases about gender, race, and religion must be brought to the surface and dealt with. If we don't deal with them, they will simmer and eventually erupt in a violent explosion of some kind.

That's what happened with the murder of George Floyd in the U.S.

Building trust among people from different parts of the world will be of paramount importance for creating an Earth Family.

I have been fortunate enough to interact with many different people and cultures. How does someone who does not travel extensively build this trust? Although there is nothing like firsthand personal experience, there are documentary and travel shows that provide a glimpse of different cultures. Many travel guides and language courses are useful in getting a glimpse of another culture. Pen-pal relationships and foreign exchange experiences provide more personal experiences. The Internet is another avenue for getting to know more about people from other countries. But of course it is rampant with false information, and caution should be used in providing personal information until trust is developed. Explore the dreams, aspirations, and fears of others. Find out what they enjoy doing.

While it is important to identify and address our prejudices and biases, that doesn't mean we all have to look alike and act alike. Cultural differences make for an interesting world. We can still have preferences for how we dress, how we worship, and for every imaginable nuance of our lives. The problem arises when we don't allow for differences in cultures, particularly when there is no harm done to other people or the planet.

Creating an Earth Family

The world is facing an extreme
either/or situation. Either we change
our behavior and work together to
address global warming and the
other issues facing us on this planet,
or we risk destroying ourselves.

We have reached a tipping point; signs of unrest and
fear are evident around the world. Elon Musk may not
have enough time to establish a sustainable society on
Mars.

What will it take for people on the planet to wake
up? Perhaps we need to think about how world citizens
would respond if the earth were suddenly besieged by
aliens from another planet. That might be the kind
of motivation we need to wake up and work better
together. As long as we have a patriarchal mindset in
charge, and the superpowers and other countries keep
building their military forces, the potential for another

world war not only is possible, but likely.

Women will need to address many issues as they take leadership over government and corporations to create a safe and nurturing world for all the earth's citizens. I recommend that a group of consultants be established to oversee the transition from patriarchal rule to women's leadership. I propose calling this group The Sages. The Sages will oversee the process of identifying and selecting the thousands of women who will become the highest-ranking leaders in governments and businesses worldwide.

To avoid the pitfall of recreating another patriarchal society, more than a majority of The Sages—two-thirds to three-fourths of the members—should be women with leadership experience and a global perspective. Men tend to dominate the interaction in a mixed group, and years of conditioning have taught women to defer to men's opinions. The men in the group need to be comfortable with having women lead; we do not want to replicate a patriarchal world, but we need the enthusiastic support of men.

One suggestion for establishing the members of The Sages would be to have a representative from the two current superpowers, the U.S. and China, along with the next most populous countries in the world: Bangladesh, Brazil, Ethiopia, India, Indonesia, Japan, Mexico, Nigeria, Pakistan, and Russia. This grouping would ensure all major races and religions would be represented, as well as provide representation from very poor and very wealthy countries. Including members from the superpowers in this group would ensure discussion with the two countries most likely to resist giving up their dominance. The Sages should consider adding the EU to this mix because of its success (although not perfect) in balancing and retaining different cultures within the EU. In spite of the recent exit of Britain and the mounting tensions between the northern and southern countries in the EU, many lessons could be offered. The inclusion of the EU would result in The Sages having thirteen members, which would enable tie-breaker voting. Most important, membership in the initial group would be based on objective criteria (population), yet allow for broad representation.

I would like to propose several women who might be included in The Sages. Dong Mingzhu, who was recently listed as one of the ten most influential businesswomen outside of the U.S., runs one of the largest appliance companies in China (Gree Electric Appliances); she would represent the second largest economy in the world and bring vast business, social, and cultural influences to the group. Andrea Merkel, the de facto leader of the EU, would bring political and scientific expertise to the group, especially in view of her leadership during the Covid-19 pandemic in Germany. As for representing the number one superpower in the world, there are several women in the U.S. who ran for the presidential nomination in 2020 and gained significant support. I suggest that Oprah Winfrey be given consideration as well; as a recognized entrepreneur in television and a non-denominational spiritual seeker, Ms. Winfrey also brings a humanitarian perspective from establishing her Oprah Winfrey Leadership Academy for Girls in South Africa.

I could name many other qualified women from around the world, but I would much rather have you nominate women that you could envision serving our world on the team of Sages. I give readers and their recommended friends and family the opportunity to nominate these leaders. At the end of this book and on my website, I provide a simple nomination form for those who wish to participate in electing the women who will be included in The Sages. I will tally the count for the nominees and inform those women who have the highest number of votes. These women can then decide how to include men in their group.

I anticipate that everything The Sages recommend and do will be done in a collaborative, compassionate, and inclusive manner. They will clarify their role and communicate to all world citizens why we need women's leadership at this time. They will explain that this is not an attempt to give women preferential treatment, but rather that women's leadership is necessary to create a better world. I would expect The Sages to emphasize and model the positive aspects of female leadership rather than feel any need to bash the patriarchal mindset.

The Sages may decide to take a worldwide poll to ascertain the amount of support for women's leadership. As of 2020, the world has slightly more males than females, with an expected sex ratio at birth of 105 males to 100 females. I would anticipate that most women in the world would vote in favor of women taking leadership over governments and corporations to create an Earth Family. Women understand that their style of leadership and skills are required to create a safe and prosperous world for all. Likewise, the younger generations and many men who are fed up with the patriarchal model would vote in favor as well. Most people in the world would welcome a change that is based on fairness and inclusivity. Many world citizens know the extraordinary talents their wives, mothers, and other women possess.

Those who will not vote for fundamental, wide-scale change in leadership will be those men and a few women in power who do not want to give up their authority. Even men and women in power who are demonstrating effective leadership will most likely support the need for massive, worldwide change. It may be a good thing that there is a small number of people in the world who have accumulated vast amounts of money and power, because there will be fewer people who see this movement to female leadership as threatening.

Let's assume that were The Sages to take a worldwide poll, the voices of the world would make it clear that they want women to lead the world. The transfer of power from a patriarchal society to women's leadership will take time ... and time is of the essence.

The Sages will need to quickly solicit analysts, assistants, and support groups to provide them with data, analysis, and alternatives for how women can take over leadership of government and business. Recommended approaches may differ in various parts of the world, based on culture and readiness for change. But with the support of world citizens, I would expect that

The Sages and their appointees will work with existing governments and corporations to find peaceful ways to transfer power to women.

I recommend that The Sages establish a team whose sole purpose would be to find ways to reduce—or ideally eliminate—the $2 trillion spent annually on defense spending. This initial work is vitally important because if that money were to be made available, much of the poverty in the world could be erased. Eliminating defense spending is actually more a psychological and sociological issue than an economic one, because most world citizens have been conditioned to believe that a large military budget equates to safety. This of course is false security.

All of the support groups need to establish rules and guidelines to discourage men from dominating the discussions and making decisions, and so that the groups do not fall back into an old, patriarchal mindset. At the same time, I cannot overstate the importance of men bringing to the table their analytical, logic-driven minds.

> Those men who have been in the shadows—who have dropped out and not wanted to participate in the patriarchal model—need to come forward and help develop a new world.

All the smart male and female scientists, doctors, and researchers must participate. One of the worst results of this effort would be if men and women were to battle each other for domination. It is important to remember that women are being put in charge of creating a new Earth Family because of their skill set.

I think it is equally important that the support groups not be comprised or heavily influenced by women who have adopted a patriarchal mindset. Many women have adopted this model so that they could succeed in business and politics. Some women in power have even shown disdain for women of a more compassionate nature. A balance of right-brain and left-brain thinking must be the hallmark of the new earth.

Input from female CEOs and women who currently lead or have led governments in the past will be valuable. Input from young people, the LGBT community, the Taliban, religious groups, and white nationalists … all facets of society must be heard.

Everyone needs to be assured a fair and safe place in the Earth Family.

The Earth needs all of us. People must not be alienated as they are today and fearful of their place in society. Above all, no one can continue to harm the planet or its inhabitants. Together with The Sages, these women and men in support groups will work together to promote new ways of thinking about global warming, universal health, wealth, poverty, business, and politics; they will provide their input to the women who will lead governments and corporations in the future.

As for the loss of innovation that some capitalistic societies may fear, the Sages and the support groups need to think of ways to promote and reward innovation and new ideas. Forms of worldwide recognition, including perks of many kinds, should be established. Imagine having your name be included to credit you as part of an international team that cured cancer and other diseases on the planet.

Some people may raise the issue that putting women in charge will lead to more wars. We heard this issue during the 2020 campaigns in the U.S. To that I say, really? After sixty-three wars, with over thirty million people killed since the end of World War II, and twenty wars still ongoing? It seems incredulous that anyone would raise such an objection. It sounds like an attempt of the patriarchy to maintain control. But it is an issue that needs to be addressed.

Other people may fear that if women are put in leadership roles, their lack of combativeness could lead to their country's demise. First, this fear sounds somewhat self-serving, and second, most countries are currently under that threat.

The Sages must consider how they will deal with military opposition, the threat of future pandemics, and global warming. Without doubt, The Sages will be eyed with suspicion, and roadblocks will be erected by some in power to thwart their progress. Hopefully, the pushback from existing leaders of governments and corporations will not be destructive, although resistance should be expected. Some powers that be will not want to relinquish their authority. Such attempts to thwart progress will need to be dealt with through a variety of diplomatic and peaceful means—not just the usual threats and combative rhetoric that many governments and corporations use to thwart any change in the status quo. I trust The Sages to address these and other concerns, and to keep reminding resistors that they have the support of world citizens.

I expect The Sages and their designees to be successful in peacefully transferring power and leadership from the patriarchy to women. Those men in the patriarchy who continue to resist a change, however, may see the writing on the wall … as Hitler did when he knew defeat was inevitable.

As more women take leadership roles in government and business, the world will see the results of a new kind of leadership. Problems not addressed for decades to create a peaceful, prosperous world for all will be resolved.

As men see the benefits produced by a new style of leadership, they will want to develop a more inclusive and egalitarian approach as well. Over time, men will develop collaborative skills and be able to assume more leadership roles. Before we know it, the world will talk about those terrible times in the past when patriarchal leadership led to war and destruction.

The question before us is this: Will we act now to establish a better world, or wait for the earth to be destroyed? This is not doomsday talk. It is a very real threat that is likely to happen unless we take action now. It might be a bomb, a pandemic, or global warming.

All it would take is a few individuals with ill-intent to destroy the planet. But it will take every citizen and nation in the world to create a new Earth Family.

The choice is ours.

Nomination Form

If you wish to help establish the group of Sages, please complete a copy of this nomination form on my website: www.RenaissanceDonna.com.

You will be able to nominate up to three women from the following list of countries: Bangladesh, Brazil, China, Ethiopia, India, Indonesia, Japan, Mexico, Nigeria, Pakistan, Russia, the U.S., and any country within the European Union.

Note: It is not necessary to purchase this book in order to nominate women for The Sages. The reader has my permission to inform family and friends about our effort, and direct them to my website. However, only one form per person should be submitted.

_____

1st Nominee: Name

_____

Nominee's Country of Residence

_____

2nd Nominee: Name

_____

Nominee's Country of Residence

_____

3rd Nominee: Name

_____

Nominee's Country of Residence

Updates about our progress toward establishing an Earth Family will be provided periodically on my website.

Other Titles by Donna Fridrych

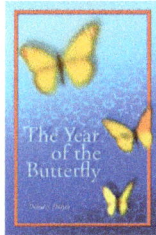

The Year of the Butterfly

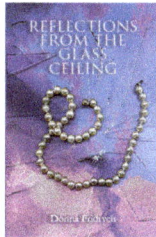

Reflections from the Glass Ceiling

RenaissanceDonna.com

About the Author

DONNA FRIDRYCH was one of the first women consultants in the field of computer technology. Starting as a computer programmer, she climbed the corporate ladder to act as Chief Information Officer for United Airlines, and later became CEO of the United Airlines Employees' Credit Union. As a marketing director, she traveled around the world conducting business in many foreign countries and relished the opportunity to get to know people from different cultures. As an entrepreneur, she owned an antique business in a four-story Victorian house for twenty years, and was also co-owner of a day spa. True to the "Renaissance Woman" label given to her by friends, she is the author of six other books, two of which are expected to be published shortly.

Donna currently spends winters in Arizona and summers at her lake home in northern Illinois with her long-term partner William and their two dogs—Valentino (Tino), who got his name when he was rescued on Valentine's Day, and Natasha (Tasha) his adorable playmate.

www.ingramcontent.com/pod-product-compliance
Lightning Source LLC
Chambersburg PA
CBHW040931050426
42334CB00060B/3197